IMAGES
of America

BOSTON'S
CENTRAL ARTERY

Looking South from near North Station, May 1954. The Central Artery viaduct is shown under construction near North Washington Street in the city's North End. In the upper right corner is a swath of cleared land. (Courtesy State Transportation Library.)

IMAGES
of America

BOSTON'S
CENTRAL ARTERY

Yanni Tsipis

ARCADIA
PUBLISHING

Published by Arcadia Publishing
Charleston, South Carolina

Library of Congress Catalog Card Number: 00110175

For all general information contact Arcadia Publishing at:
Telephone 843-853-2070
Fax 843-853-0044
E-mail sales@arcadiapublishing.com
For customer service and orders:
Toll-Free 1-888-313-2665

Visit us on the Internet at www.arcadiapublishing.com

DEMOLITION WORK NEAR DEWEY SQUARE, SPRING 1957. For nearly three years, Bostonians lived with a 200-foot-wide, 40-foot-deep trench that ran a half mile through the southwestern part of downtown. (Courtesy the Barletta Company.)

CONTENTS

ACKNOWLEDGMENTS

Much attention in Boston and the surrounding region is currently focused on the Central Artery/Tunnel project, popularly called the Big Dig. This book looks back at the city's first Big Dig—the construction of the original Central Artery in the 1950s.

This book would not have been possible without the generosity and assistance of the following: Tim Barletta at the Barletta Company, Sean O'Neill and Dennis Rahilly at the Central Artery/Tunnel project, Cranston Rogers at the Maguire Group Inc., Fred Salvucci at the MIT Center for Transportation Studies, Aaron Schmidt at the Boston Public Library's Print Department, Amy Sutton and Megan Dumm at Arcadia Publishing, and Peter Vanderwarker.

I would like to give special thanks to George Sanborn at the State Transportation Library. His constant encouragement and assistance drove this book forward from its inception.

—Yanni Tsipis, Massachusetts Institute of Technology
Cambridge, Massachusetts

INTRODUCTION

Late in 1925, a committee convened by the Massachusetts state legislature submitted its final report detailing measures meant to address "intolerable conditions" associated with the "street problem in down-town Boston." Even at a time when only one in five Boston area residents owned a car, traffic conditions on the city's narrow and winding downtown streets were rapidly deteriorating. The report recommended the construction of a major north-south thoroughfare through the city, intended to "open up parts of the down-town district" and "give general traffic relief." Although the recommendation met with legislative approval after the completion of a more detailed study in 1930, the onset of the Great Depression and the outbreak of World War II prevented the plans from moving forward.

The early years of postwar prosperity saw renewed emphasis on highway projects in and around Boston. In 1947, Gov. Robert Bradford commissioned a detailed study of potential highway projects in the Boston metropolitan area. The resultant 1948 Highway Master Plan became the most influential transportation planning document of the 20th century for Boston and its surrounding region. Among other things, it detailed the alignment and design of a major expressway through the city, designed to distribute traffic coming into downtown onto the city's network of streets. Although the 1948 plan made the phrase "Central Artery" part of the city's permanent vernacular, the term had been coined in the second decade of the 20th century to describe a proposed mass transit link between North and South Stations. The rail link was never built, but the term was easily adapted to a vehicular expressway that would follow a similar route.

In 1948, Republican Governor Bradford asked the state legislature to authorize a massive bond issue to back the 1948 Highway Master Plan in cash. A solidly Democratic legislature stalled the issue until Democrat Paul Dever was elected to the governorship in November. Dever reappointed longtime Democratic stalwart William F. Callahan as commissioner of public works after an 11-year hiatus, and the legislature promptly authorized an issue of $100 million for highway projects, paid for by a 3¢-per-gallon gasoline tax. Over the next few years, subsequent authorizations (paid for by further tax increases) added another $350 million to the state's highway coffers. Although a huge list of highway projects had been generated by the 1948 Highway Master Plan, the first priority of the Massachusetts Department of Public Works (DPW) was to build the Central Artery through Boston. Over the next decade, nearly a quarter of all highway dollars spent in the state went to its construction.

Work on the Central Artery began with the crash of a wrecking ball near the corner of

Beverly and North Washington Streets in the North End in the fall of 1951. Property takings and evictions had begun in 1950, and a cloud of impending disaster wafted gradually over the city's oldest and most cohesive residential neighborhood. Several of the images in this book capture merchants in their last days of business before being demolished by the Central Artery work. A swath of destruction slowly worked its way south through the commercial heart of the North End and then into the downtown core. Progress was slowed by holdouts: Haymarket meat merchants delayed their eviction until new quarters had been furnished; one tenant of the small commercial row building at 200 Milk Street held up demolition in that area for a month before vacating; work halted for a week near Fulton Street in the North End after a boy who had been playing amid the wrecked buildings was injured. By the fall of 1953, however, the demolition had progressed as far south as Oliver Street, near Fort Hill Square.

Construction of the Central Artery viaduct began in the city's Bulfinch Triangle area just east of North Station. By the summer of 1954, the massive steel roadway was taking shape through the North End. As construction proceeded, however, opposition to the project's proposed southern section had caused DPW Commissioner John Volpe to reconsider his plans. Originally, the Central Artery was to snake its way south from Fort Hill Square through the city's leather district and Chinatown as an elevated structure. As residents in the path of the proposed right-of-way saw firsthand the effect that the elevated structure would have on the North End, support grew for a proposal to put the remainder of the Central Artery in a tunnel. In the winter of 1953, Volpe commissioned reports detailing the various proposals for the southern route. In May 1954, he decided to place the section of the Central Artery from Congress Street to Kneeland Street underground, sparing the southern neighborhoods the blight of the elevated expressway. Once the decision had been made, demolition began south of Fort Hill Square. Construction of the tunnel lasted nearly three years and was completed on June 25, 1959. The date was crucial; only a week later, the New Haven railroad cut off its commuter rail service to the south after losing its state subsidy for the service.

The construction of the Central Artery through Boston marked the beginning of a two-decade-long program of highway construction and urban renewal that drastically changed the shape of the city. It also had more subtle effects; within a few years of the Central Artery's inauguration, the New Haven railroad went bankrupt as truck transport became the mode of choice for Boston's commercial sector. Exactly three months after the Central Artery opened, a minor accident north of the city backed up afternoon rush-hour traffic all the way to Fort Hill Square. As months turned into years and decades, even accident-free rush hours turned into half-hour crawls through the city. By the mid-1970s—barely 15 years after being opened to traffic—plans were already being formulated to rid the city of the elevated expressway. Today, the city is in the midst of its most complex engineering endeavor, a project that will put the elevated portion of the Central Artery underground and reknit the fabric of the city.

One

BOSTON BEFORE THE ARTERY

THE OPEN-AIR MARKET ALONG BLACKSTONE STREET IN THE CITY'S NORTH END. Delmar's Restaurant, at the corner of Blackstone and North Streets, is now the site of the Bostonian Hotel. The entire block along the right side of Blackstone Street was demolished to make way for the Central Artery. In the distance is the Haymarket Relief Hospital, built in 1901. (Courtesy CA/T Archives.)

BOSTON BEFORE THE CENTRAL ARTERY. The city's dense North End lies in the foreground, while the curving spine of commercial and office buildings lines Atlantic Avenue along the city's bustling waterfront (far left). North Station lies to the far right, and South Station is on

the far left. The Custom House Tower is one of a only a handful of structures over ten stories tall. Skyscrapers were slow in coming to Boston, and not until the mid-1960s did the city's skyline change dramatically. (Courtesy CA/T Archives.)

VIEW FROM THE WARREN BRIDGE, SEPTEMBER 1951. The Warren Bridge was the major traffic artery into the city from the north before the construction of the Central Artery. On the right is the massive North Station Industrial (later Anelex) Building, built in 1928 by the Boston and Maine Railroad. This view was taken on a weekend afternoon, but on weekdays the bridge was jammed with vehicles entering the city. (Courtesy the Barletta Company.)

LOOKING SOUTH FROM CHARLESTOWN ACROSS THE CHARLES RIVER TOWARD THE NORTH STATION INDUSTRIAL BUILDING, OCTOBER 1951. The Warren Bridge is just out of frame to the right. In the background is the Tidewater Terminal Storage building. Built in 1901, the building was soon partially demolished to make way for the Central Artery. (STL.)

LOOKING NORTH ALONG BEVERLY STREET TOWARD THE WARREN BRIDGE, FALL 1951.
This photograph gives a good view of the ornate Tidewater Terminal Storage building. Also prominent is the city's first transportation-related elevated structure, the Forest Hills–Everett elevated railway, seen here over Causeway Street. (Courtesy the Barletta Company.)

BLACKSTONE STREET, SEPTEMBER 1951. Of particular note in this view are the signs in the windows of Craft's Bargain Center: "Forced Out for New Overhead Arterial Highway," "Forced Out of Business to Make Room for New Highway," and "Building Coming Down—Forced to Vacate." Demolition of this area began in the early spring of 1952. (Courtesy the Barletta Company.)

LOOKING SOUTH DOWN BLACKSTONE STREET FROM HANOVER STREET. Delmar's Restaurant is at the end of the block on the right. The entire block on the left side of Blackstone Street has only months to live. (Courtesy the Barletta Company.)

LOOKING NORTH UP BLACKSTONE STREET FROM HANOVER STREET IN FRONT OF GRAY'S SUPERMARKET. The late afternoon sun illuminates the doomed block of buildings along the right side of the street. The Haymarket Relief Hospital is visible at the far side of Haymarket Square. (Courtesy the Barletta Company.)

LOOKING WEST ACROSS CROSS STREET UP HANOVER STREET TOWARD THE SUFFOLK COUNTY COURTHOUSE, FALL 1951. This block of buildings between Cross Street and Blackstone Street was demolished about six months after this photograph was taken. Already signs of the block's demise are evident—Epstein's Drugstore has been vacated and plastered with posters. (Courtesy the Barletta Company.)

HANOVER STREET, LOOKING WEST FROM THE INTERSECTION WITH BLACKSTONE STREET, FALL 1951. The Gray store in the upper right corner was the neighborhood's major supermarket. Although it survived the Central Artery construction, this entire block of Hanover Street was razed a decade later as part of the Scollay Square/Government Center urban renewal project. (Courtesy the Barletta Company.)

15

BLACKSTONE STREET AT THE HEIGHT OF THE OPEN-AIR MARKET. Residents from all parts of the city flocked to Haymarket on Saturday mornings to take advantage of the market, but North

Enders dominated. Located in the heart of their neighborhood, the market for North Enders was as much a social event as it was a shopping trip. (Courtesy the Barletta Company.)

LOOKING NORTH TOWARD HAYMARKET SQUARE. This unique panorama looks across Hanover Street and shows, from left to right, Blackstone Street, Endicott Street, and Salem Street. With the exception of the block along the left side of Blackstone Street and the Haymarket Relief

Hospital at the end of Blackstone Street, every building in this view was destroyed by Central Artery construction. (Courtesy the Barletta Company.)

LOOKING SOUTHEAST FROM HIGH ABOVE HAYMARKET SQUARE, C. 1950. Cross Street, widened in 1933, is visible in front of the entrance to the Sumner Tunnel in the lower left corner. The Central Artery demolished the entire block of buildings at the bottom center of the image, between Cross Street and Blackstone Street. It continued south between Quincy Market and the low buildings of the city's wholesale produce and meat district. (Courtesy CA/T Archives.)

CROSS STREET. This view shows a sign pointing north toward the Sumner Tunnel. Cross Street was one of the city's major traffic thoroughfares before Central Artery construction and was the most direct route to Logan Airport, the northern suburbs, and interstate points up U.S. Route 1. (Courtesy the Barletta Company.)

Looking East along Cross Street at the Base of the Colonial Meat Products Building from near the Sumner Tunnel Entrance. The block on the far side of the street was demolished soon after this photograph was taken. The buildings in the foreground on the near side survived another decade before being razed to make way for the Callahan Tunnel. (Courtesy the Barletta Company.)

Boston's Commercial District c. 1950. The path of the expressway swooped in from the upper right corner of this view, curved at Mercantile Street on the lower right, and passed through the heart of the commercial district. It cut a broad swath roughly parallel to the bottom of the image just in front of Quincy Market and the Custom House Tower. (Courtesy CA/T Archives.)

THE CITY'S WATERFRONT BEFORE THE ARTERY. This *c.* 1940 view shows, from left to right, Rowes Wharf, India Wharf, Central Wharf, and Long Wharf. Most of the dockage is owned by the Eastern Steamship Corporation, with the exception of Long Wharf, which served the United Fruit Company. The old Atlantic Avenue elevated railway is visible just inland. (Courtesy CA/T Archives.)

LOOKING WEST ACROSS THE CITY, C. 1930. At the bottom center of this view is the Rowes Wharf block fronting on Atlantic Avenue. The U.S. Appraisers Stores building, built in 1917, sits at the corner of Northern Avenue and Atlantic Avenue on the left. The Atlantic Avenue elevated railway viaduct is visible, and the Custom House Tower monopolizes the city skyline. (Courtesy CA/T Archives.)

DEWEY SQUARE, C. 1950. This northerly view, taken from the top of South Station, shows the block of office buildings along the western side of Atlantic Avenue. All of these buildings were demolished as the Central Artery tunnel ate up the block between Atlantic Avenue and Purchase Street in 1956. (Courtesy CA/T Archives.)

LOOKING NORTHWEST FROM ABOVE SOUTH STATION, C. 1930. This view shows much of the city's wool and leather district before the Central Artery tore a path running from Dewey Square (lower right) diagonally across the center of the image before curving behind the Lincoln Building (center left). (Courtesy CA/T Archives.)

THE CHINESE MERCHANTS ASSOCIATION BUILDING BEFORE PARTIAL DEMOLITION IN 1957.
Completed in 1953, the building stood along Kneeland Street between Hudson and Albany
Streets at the southwestern end of the city's Chinatown district. Chinatown centered on Beach
Street, one block to the north, and contained many buildings that housed a large portion of the
city's clothing manufacturing industries. (Courtesy CA/T Archives.)

Two

THE ARTERY UNDER CONSTRUCTION

EXCAVATION ON CROSS STREET IN FRONT OF THE SUMNER TUNNEL ENTRANCE IN THE NORTH END. Cross Street became one of the city's busiest traffic thoroughfares after being widened in 1933 to accommodate tunnel traffic. The tunnel's toll booth is visible on the right. (Courtesy the Barletta Company.)

Looking North from the Haymarket Relief Hospital Building, December 1951. Demolition work in the city began along the block between North Washington and Haverhill Streets in the fall of 1951 and began eating into the city's North End. The intersection of Haverhill and North Washington Streets is in the foreground. (Courtesy the Barletta Company.)

The Same View Less Than a Month Later. The entire block has been razed and cleared in this photograph. Focus has shifted farther up North Washington Street to Beverly Street, where several industrial loft buildings are next in line. The Tidewater Terminal Storage building is visible in the upper left corner. (Courtesy the Barletta Company.)

26

A Loft Building on Beverly Street Being Razed, Early 1952. Although their view would soon be obscured once again by the Central Artery's viaduct, residents in the apartment building on the right were afforded a few years of light and air (and construction noise) as this warehouse was torn down. (Courtesy the Barletta Company.)

Beverly Street a Few Months Later. In this view, the entire block along Beverly Street has been demolished and the Tidewater Terminal Storage building in the background is coming down. In the distance, the elevated railway viaduct is visible running east over Causeway Street before turning north toward Charlestown on North Washington Street. (Courtesy the Barletta Company.)

LOOKING SOUTH ALONG BEVERLY STREET, SEPTEMBER 1951. The elevated railway looms overhead as loft buildings are demolished in the background. This area, known as the Bulfinch Triangle, was laid out and partially built up by Boston's famous native architect Charles Bulfinch in the early 1800s. It was home to many handsome old brick warehouse and industrial loft buildings before the Central Artery tore a swath between Haverhill and Medford Streets. (Courtesy the Barletta Company.)

LOOKING SOUTH ALONG BEVERLY STREET TOWARD NORTH WASHINGTON STREET. The extent of the demolition is apparent in this view looking under the elevated railway structure. Note the streetcar tracks laid in Beverly and Causeway Streets. (Courtesy the Barletta Company.)

DRIVING PILES FOR THE ARTERY'S FOUNDATION IN THE BOSTON AND MAINE RAILROAD YARDS, SPRING 1952. The completed Charles River crossing stands ready to meet the new Artery in this view. Charlestown's City Square, just visible on the right, has yet to be overshadowed by a massive off ramp that loomed over South Charlestown for decades before being torn down in the early stages of the current Central Artery/Tunnel project. The Bunker Hill Monument is visible at far right. (Courtesy the Barletta Company.)

DRIVING CONCRETE PILES BETWEEN BEVERLY AND HAVERHILL STREETS, WINTER 1952. The elevated railway structure can be seen on the left emerging from under Haymarket Square and curving east on Causeway Street with North Station and the Boston Garden in the background. The piles stood under the Central Artery's steel support columns and concrete strip footings. (Courtesy the Barletta Company.)

LOOKING NORTH FROM CROSS STREET, JUNE 1952. The dirt roadway in the bottom right corner eventually became the Haymarket Square off ramp, serving the Sumner Tunnel. In this view, workers are erecting the formwork for the concrete walls of the earth-filled ramp. (Courtesy the Barletta Company.)

DEMOLITION OF A RETAIL AND WAREHOUSE BUILDING AT THE CORNER OF BEVERLY AND NORTH WASHINGTON STREETS, DECEMBER 30, 1951. This photograph gives only a small idea of what the city's North End would suffer through in 1952. Up to this point, most of the buildings cleared had been warehouse structures. Over the next several months, the Central Artery would tear through the city's oldest and most cohesive residential neighborhood. (Courtesy the Barletta Company.)

DEMOLITION OF THE HAYMARKET BLOCK AT THE CORNER OF NORTH WASHINGTON AND STILLMAN STREETS, MARCH 1952. The signs in the windows indicate that the street-level business has relocated to a space nearby on the other side of Haymarket Square. Many businesses were not so lucky and had to move out of the neighborhood altogether. Many closed their doors for good. (Courtesy the Barletta Company.)

LOOKING ACROSS CROSS STREET FROM THE SUMNER TUNNEL ENTRANCE, FEBRUARY 1952. No fewer than three demolition contractors worked simultaneously to bring down pieces of the old neighborhood. Officials at the Massachusetts Department of Public Works emphasized that speed was crucial to the project, but many North Enders maintain that along with buildings, a fair public process and equitable compensation were bulldozed in the interest of speeding the roadway into construction. (Courtesy the Barletta Company.)

NORTH WASHINGTON STREET AT CROSS STREET, FEBRUARY 1952. This view shows buildings along North Washington Street that have been gutted and have only a month to live. This block housed a series of food service and retail equipment dealers and several small professional offices. (Courtesy the Barletta Company.)

THE SAME BLOCK A MONTH LATER. Haymarket Square is visible on the far right. (Courtesy the Barletta Company.)

THE NORTH WASHINGTON STREET BLOCK, LATE SPRING 1952. In this view, the block is almost completely demolished. Playbills have been pasted on all the flat surfaces that remain standing. In the following decade, scenes like this one were much repeated in the city of Boston.

34

The Central Artery construction was just the first of a series of large projects that gutted some of the city's oldest and densest residential neighborhoods. (Courtesy the Barletta Company.)

THE CORNER OF HANOVER AND SALEM STREETS, SPRING 1952. Once the site of the Direct Shoe Market, the corner has been reduced to rubble. Note the ornate buildings on the opposite side of Salem Street—soon to meet a similar fate. (Courtesy the Barletta Company.)

DRIVING PILES AMID THE RUBBLE AT THE CORNER OF NORTH WASHINGTON AND STILLMAN STREETS. Demolition proceeds in the background of this photograph, taken in the spring of 1952. Above the ruins of the city's oldest residential neighborhood stands the Custom House Tower, completed in 1915.

A Lone Onlooker Examining the Demolition on Hanover Street near the Old Post Office, February 1952. North End residents recall that the demolition in their neighborhood happened so quickly that it proved impossible for many to make adequate relocation plans in advance of the bulldozers. Many displaced residents moved to the nearby West End, which was also razed barely a decade later. (Courtesy the Barletta Company.)

DEMOLITION OF THE EASTERN MASSACHUSETTS STREET RAILWAY COMPANY HEADQUARTERS AND BUS TERMINAL AT HAYMARKET SQUARE, JUNE 1952. Located at the end of Cross Street between Endicott and Blackstone Streets, this was Boston's northern terminal for many intercity bus routes. The corporate offices of the Eastern Massachusetts Street Railway Company were located on the upper floors. (Courtesy the Barletta Company.)

BUILDINGS ON THE NORTHERN SIDE OF HAYMARKET SQUARE COMING DOWN, SUMMER 1952. The rotary at Haymarket Square was one of the city's worst traffic bottlenecks. A pedestrian underpass (lower left) was added to the existing subway station to reduce pedestrian injuries and deaths. Cross Street is visible on the right. (Courtesy the Barletta Company.)

LOOKING EAST PAST HAYMARKET SQUARE AND A CLEARED LOT UP CROSS STREET, SUMMER 1952. Cross Street had been widened in 1933 to provide better access to the new Sumner Tunnel, which opened in 1934. (Courtesy the Barletta Company.)

THE INTERSECTION OF HANOVER AND CROSS STREETS, 1952. Compare this view to the one at the top of page 15, taken from a similar vantage point. Note the horse-drawn cart at center on Cross Street. (Courtesy the Barletta Company.)

TRAFFIC ON HANOVER STREET WITH SALEM STREET IN THE FOREGROUND, SPRING 1952. This area had once been the heart of the North End. Although the Central Artery was meant to ease traffic on the streets of downtown, the years of its construction were characterized by frequent gridlock as many local streets were closed and reshaped. (Courtesy the Barletta Company.)

THE FACE OF DEFIANCE ON BLACKSTONE STREET, SPRING 1952. As the neighborhood comes down around her, a North End shopkeeper conducts business as usual—with appropriate skepticism. Even with construction proceeding only a few steps in front of their shops, storekeepers along Blackstone and Cross Streets stayed open through the years of accompanying noise, dust, and vibrations. (Photograph by Leslie Jones; courtesy Boston Public Library, Prints Department.)

A Northerly View from the Custom House Tower, Early Spring 1952. With much of the North End's commercial district still intact, a swath of cleared land is visible in the Bulfinch Triangle area (upper left). Since the main market area along Blackstone Street (left of center) is occupied by cars, it must be a weekday. In the lower right corner is the light-colored Whitney Building. (Photograph by Leslie Jones; courtesy Boston Public Library, Prints Department.)

The Same View Eight Months Later. The Whitney Building is being demolished, and the block just to its north is next. A construction superintendent's log entry written during the demolition of that block reads, "Corner of North and John—4 stories collapsed in 8 minutes." (Photograph by Leslie Jones; courtesy Boston Public Library, Prints Department.)

LOOKING NORTH IN THE VICINITY OF HANOVER STREET FROM BLACKSTONE STREET, APRIL 1954. Once the lots had been cleared of rubble, work could begin on the Central Artery's structure. Salem Street can be seen extending into the North End at the center of the photograph. (STL.)

HAYMARKET SQUARE, APRIL 1954. This view, looking northwest from Blackstone Street, shows the extent of demolition. North Station is visible at top left, as is the Federalist-style Haymarket Relief Hospital, built in 1901 on the site of the old Eastern (later Boston and Maine) Railroad terminal. In the foreground, steel girders and beams lie in storage. (STL.)

LOOKING EAST FROM HAYMARKET SQUARE, SPRING 1954. Almost two years after demolition of this area was completed, the Central Artery's steel viaduct is finally taking shape. Ironwork was subcontracted to both a fabricator—Mount Vernon—and a field erector—New England Erecting. (STL.)

NORTHERLY VIEW FROM HAYMARKET SQUARE, MAY 1954. This view shows the steel viaduct being erected between Cross and Blackstone Streets. Shops along Cross Street are visible in the background. (STL.)

CENTRAL ARTERY WORK IN THE VICINITY OF NORTH STATION. This view looks north toward Charlestown with the completed Charles River Bridge on the left. The elevated viaduct splits at this point to meet the bridge's upper (northbound) and lower (southbound) decks. The

City Square ramp now casts its shadow over Charlestown in the background. On the right is the North Washington Street Bridge, with the Forest Hills–Everett elevated railway viaduct running over it. (STL.)

LOOKING SOUTH AT THE ARTERY VIADUCT FROM THE CHARLES RIVER BRIDGE, SPRING 1954. The North Station Industrial Building is visible on the right, and the truncated Tidewater Terminal Storage building is on the left. The Storrow Drive ramp swings west under the Central Artery's main viaduct, and Beverly Street disappears under the massive structure in the lower left corner. (Courtesy Cranston Rogers.)

THE FIRST LINK BETWEEN BOSTON AND THE NEW EXPRESSWAY TO THE NORTH BEING HOISTED INTO PLACE, SPRING 1954. The Charles River crossing was contracted separately from the Boston portion of the Central Artery. It was completed in 1953 by the Berke Moore Company. (Courtesy Cranston Rogers.)

LOOKING WEST ALONG CAUSEWAY STREET, SPRING 1954. With the Central Artery's steel skeleton now nearly complete, an Everett-bound elevated trolley makes its way toward North Washington Street. The elevated tracks were removed in 1975, leaving the Central Artery towering over Causeway Street at this point. (STL.)

THE DOUBLE-DECKER STORROW DRIVE CONNECTOR RAMP BEHIND THE BOSTON GARDEN. Visible in the upper left corner is the Hotel Manger at 80 Causeway Street, adjacent to North Station. One of the most fashionable hotels in the city, it was sold only a few years after this picture was taken. It was demolished in the 1970s to make way for the current Tip O'Neill Federal Building. (STL.)

LOOKING NORTH TOWARD CHARLESTOWN AT THE ALMOST COMPLETED NORTHERN SECTION OF THE ARTERY, JULY 1954. In this view, the massive double-deck interchange towers over the old Warren Bridge, today the site of the Charles River Dam. The original Warren Bridge was built in 1828. It was the focus of the famous legal case brought by the proprietors of the neighboring Charles River (now North Washington Street) Bridge, visible at right. (STL.)

LOOKING NORTH FROM THE TOP OF THE NORTH STATION INDUSTRIAL BUILDING, JULY 1954. This area comprised one of the most complex highway interchanges in the world at the time it was built. (STL.)

LOOKING SOUTH FROM THE LOWER DECK OF THE CHARLES RIVER BRIDGE, JULY 1954. In this view, steel reinforcing has been installed, and platforms for concrete finishers lie ready for the roadway deck to be poured. The Storrow Drive ramp curves off to the right. (STL.)

WORKERS NEAR THE NORTH STATION INDUSTRIAL BUILDING. Workers are laying sheets of asphalt-waterproofing material over the top of the concrete roadway deck just before paving it with blacktop. To the right is the double-deck roadway just south of the Charles River Bridge. (STL.)

LOOKING NORTHWEST OVER THE BOSTON AND MAINE RAILROAD YARDS AT NORTH STATION. The elevated Storrow Drive ramps passed over the Boston and Maine Railroad yards on their way to Leverett Circle, on the far side of the DPW headquarters building at 100 Nashua Street. A Boston Edison plant is to the left of 100 Nashua Street, and a sliver of the old West End neighborhood is just visible in the upper left corner. (STL.)

FOUNDATION WORK ON THE LEVERETT CIRCLE RAMPS NEAR NASHUA STREET. Workers are placing a section of concrete strip footing, which will support a retaining wall similar to the one being covered with black waterproofing sheets in the background. (STL.)

LOOKING SOUTH FROM ABOVE CAUSEWAY STREET, APRIL 1954. By the spring of 1954, the Central Artery was nearly completed north of Haymarket Square. Haverhill Street is on the right in this view. Tracks for the Lechmere branch of the Metropolitan Transit Authority (MTA) as well as the Forest Hills–Everett elevated line can be seen emerging from under Haymarket Square on the opposite side of the street. (STL.)

THE SAME VIEW TWO MONTHS LATER. Two elevated trains are just visible in the lower right corner. On the extreme right, a pair of Brookline-Lechmere PCC cars is heading south. Two tracks to the left is a northbound Forest Hills–Everett train. The Central Artery has now reached Hanover Street in the distance. (STL.)

LOOKING NORTH PAST THE NORTH STATION INDUSTRIAL BUILDING, APRIL 1954. Workers are placing supports for a latticework of steel reinforcing bars for the roadway deck just before they pour the concrete. (STL.)

PLACING THE CONCRETE ROADWAY DECK NEAR NORTH WASHINGTON STREET, APRIL 1954. On the right, the third-floor windows of the Medford Street apartment buildings are just yards from the expressway deck. Despite the rather unpleasant view these windows now face, they previously faced a dim air shaft at the middle of the Beverly Street–Medford Street block—until the Beverly Street half was razed. (STL.)

Looking South in the Vicinity of Cross Street, July 1954. Engineers pose with their work, oblivious to the havoc it has wrought on the neighborhood behind them. The small shops along Cross Street in the background once faced a bustling commercial district. The Artery took the opposite side of the street and cut off the entire neighborhood from Scollay Square. (STL.)

Looking South toward Downtown over the Southbound Haymarket Square Off Ramp, July 1954. The North Market Building of Quincy Market is clearly visible on the right. (STL.)

THE STEEL SKELETON OF THE ARTERY TAKING SHAPE, JULY 1954. Blackstone Street is in the lower right corner of this image. Just visible in the center is the Colonial Revival–style Tunnel Administration Building on North Street at the entrance to the Sumner Tunnel. Of particular note are the ascending piece numbers painted on the guardrail sections that have been installed

on the main viaduct section. These numbers simplified the process of installation. When delivered to the field, the steel pieces sported a shop coat of bright orange paint. Only later was the entire structure painted green. (STL.)

LOOKING SOUTH FROM HANOVER STREET, JULY 1954. In this image, a vast expanse of steel dwarfs the city. Today this view is much changed, but high-rise construction in the city's downtown area did not begin in earnest until the late 1960s. From the time of its completion in 1915 until the Prudential tower was completed in 1964, the Custom House Tower remained the tallest structure in the city. (STL.)

LOOKING SOUTH ALONG THE ALMOST COMPLETE NORTHERN SECTION OF THE ARTERY, JULY 1954. This photograph, taken a few blocks north of the preceding one, shows the concrete formwork laid atop the Artery's steel framework. In the foreground is a sawtooth expansion joint, which allows sections of the roadway to move slightly relative to one another. (STL.)

THE CONSTRUCTION ALONG BLACKSTONE STREET, JULY 1954. The Colonial Meats building at the corner of Cross and North Streets was home to one of the city's largest processed meat wholesalers at the time. A wide swath is visible in the distance at right where demolition has been completed, but steel has not yet been put up. (STL.)

HOISTING A STEEL BOX GIRDER INTO PLACE IN FRONT OF THE SUMNER TUNNEL ENTRANCE, AUGUST 1954. Atop the beam, ironworkers hammer in drift pins in order to hold the massive girder in position before being permanently riveted to the columns that support it. In the lower left corner, a crowd of onlookers has gathered to observe the work. (Courtesy Peter Vanderwarker.)

MARKET DAY, OCTOBER 1, 1954. This view from a rooftop on Commercial Street shows the crowded open-air produce and fish market along the western side of Blackstone Street. Despite the construction, the market is still packed. Note the southbound entrance ramp in the foreground and the wall it creates in front of Cross Street. The Art Deco tower on the left is the Suffolk County Courthouse, built in 1936. (STL.)

ANOTHER VIEW TWO MONTHS LATER. Steel erection is being completed, and the amputation of the North End from the rest of the city is nearly a *fait accompli*. The section of the Central Artery to the north is already in service to and from the Sumner Tunnel. (STL.)

AN IRONWORKER CORRECTING BOLT HOLE SIZES IN STRUCTURAL STEEL. The parallel rows of steel brackets in the center of this photograph support the roadway's sawtooth expansion joints, which allow neighboring sections of roadway to move slightly relative to each other. (STL.)

THE NEARLY COMPLETE EXIT RAMP PASSING OVER NORTH WASHINGTON STREET, JULY 1954. This ramp took the place of the Haymarket Block, shown at the top of page 32. (STL.)

THE CROSS STREET EXIT RAMP, NOVEMBER 1954. This photograph shows the complex snow-melting system that lay under the roadway on Central Artery ramps. The system worked by pumping steam-heated brine through the latticework of small pipes just below the roadway surface. In practice, it was found that the system worked only when turned on long before any expected snowfall or icing. (STL.)

POURING AND FINISHING CONCRETE JUST SOUTH OF HAYMARKET SQUARE, JULY 1955. This southbound entry ramp originally ran from Dock Square around the back of the North Market Building at North Street. It lasted only a few years before being torn down. (STL.)

LOOKING SOUTH ALONG BLACKSTONE STREET, SEPTEMBER 1955. North Enders shop for produce as workers reset a manhole cover in the foreground. Note the trickle of shoppers passing under the Artery viaduct. The DPW was slow to resurface areas adjacent to the Central Artery, and muddy lots such as this one remained long after the construction had been completed. (STL.)

THE VIEW FROM UNDER THE ARTERY, DECEMBER 1954. With construction work nearly completed, the full impact of the Central Artery's presence became apparent. This barren and ominous streetscape now separated the entire North End from the rest of the city. The southern end of Hanover Street, formerly the North End's commercial and transportation axis, had been cut off and would soon fall victim to urban renewal. (STL.)

A Lone Demolition Worker atop the Remainder of the Whitney Building at the Corner of Clinton and Commercial Streets, Fall 1952. Given the close proximity of surrounding buildings, much of the demolition work had to proceed by hand. Of particular note in this view is the variety of architectural ornamentation that made the Whitney Building one of the city's finest examples of early-20th-century commercial architecture. (Photograph by Leslie Jones; courtesy Boston Public Library, Prints Department.)

THE VIEW FROM THE CUSTOM HOUSE TOWER, SEPTEMBER 1954. Concrete ramp walls are being formed amid a sea of rubble. Three downtown streets have been cut off. They are, from left to right, South Market, Commerce, and State Streets. Beyond the demolition is the city's wholesale produce and meat district, dominated by the Clinton Beef Wholesale Market in the center. The wholesale district was cleared in the early 1970s and became Christopher Columbus Park. (STL.)

THE LANDSCAPE LEFT AFTER DEMOLITION, JULY 1954. Concrete footings for the steel viaduct structure stud the ground along with reconstructed manholes that allow access to the maze of relocated utility lines crisscrossing under the new roadway. This space had been occupied by a row of six-story brick professional buildings between State and Commerce Streets. (STL.)

WORKERS APPLYING TAR WATERPROOFING TO STEEL BASE PLATES, JULY 1954. The anchor bolts welded to these plates were passed through drilled plates at the bottom of each steel viaduct column, forming a steel foot, which in turn rested on a concrete pad sunk into the earth. (STL.)

UTILITY RELOCATION WORK DOWNTOWN, APRIL 1955. Boston's streets contained 150 years' worth of utility pipes of varying sizes and function, many of which had to be relocated before excavation and viaduct construction. Lacking detailed records of location, contractors were left with little alternative other than to dig gingerly and relocate lines wherever they conflicted with the Central Artery's foundations. (STL.)

THE INSTALLATION OF STEAM LINES SERVING THE ARTERY'S SNOW-MELTING SYSTEM, SPRING 1955. Ultimately, the pioneering system was used for only a few years. The system worked tolerably if turned on well in advance of a snowfall or deep freeze, but the DPW had neglected to secure long-term funding to buy the steam necessary for operation from the Edison plant on Kneeland Street. During the 1950s, the DPW spent every dollar possible on new construction and made no forward accounting of maintenance costs. After a few years of limited operation, the system lapsed into disuse. (STL.)

THE VIEW FROM CLINTON STREET, DECEMBER 1954. The Boston Wholesale Grocery Company warehouse at the end of Mercantile Row near Commercial and Cross Streets suddenly found itself cut off from Quincy Market and the rest of the city as steel went up in the fall of 1954. (STL.)

LOOKING NORTH ALONG THE CROSS STREET EXTENSION, JUNE 1955. Before the opening of the Central Artery, the produce and meat wholesalers concentrated around the intersection of Commercial Street and Atlantic Avenue were served primarily by the Union Freight Railway. The Clinton Market had an indoor loading track running through its center. Once the Central Artery opened the heart of the city to convenient truck traffic, trucks took over most of the duty. (STL.)

A VIEW FROM THE CUSTOM HOUSE TOWER, OCTOBER 1954. This image shows the extent of construction in the vicinity of India Street. The six-story New England Stationary Company building once occupied the lot facing the turreted Grain and Wheat Exchange building between India and Milk Streets, but was demolished in early 1953. Atlantic Avenue is just out of view at the top of the photograph. (STL.)

FORMERLY CONTIGUOUS BLOCKS OF COMMERCIAL BUILDINGS ALONG STATE STREET (LEFT) AND CENTRAL STREET. This photograph, taken only a month after the previous one, shows how quickly the steel for the Central Artery went up as it snaked through downtown. The row buildings in the foreground survive today. (STL.)

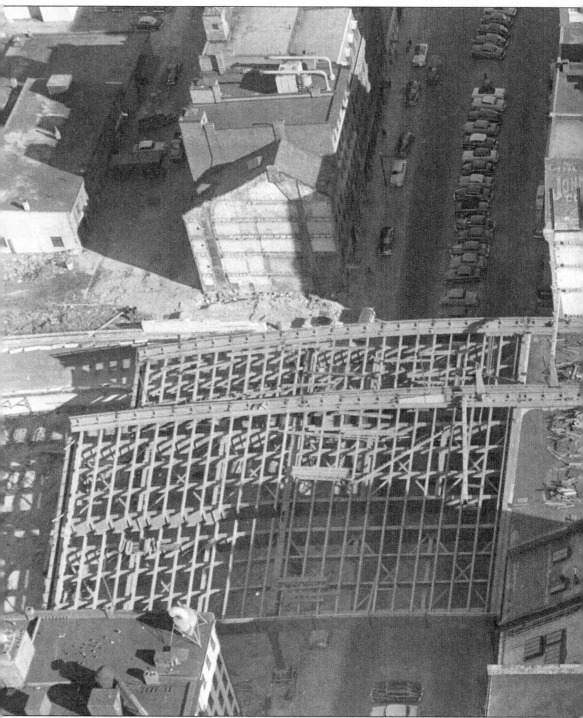

THE VIEW FROM THE CUSTOM HOUSE TOWER, JANUARY 1955. Erection of the middle section from State Street to Commercial Street had begun only two months before this photograph was taken, more than two years after demolition in this area had been completed. The blank facade of 221 State Street bears the scars left by the demolition of its neighbor. The outline of

the walls, interior floors and chimneys of 217 State Street are evident, as are the white-painted walls that were once on the interior of the building. All of the buildings on the far side of the Artery came down 15 years later, when Atlantic Avenue was relocated farther inland. (STL.)

A GROUND-LEVEL VIEW OF THE PIECE OF ROADWAY FROM STATE STREET TO COMMERCIAL STREET. The Central Artery viaduct was built in sections, not necessarily contiguously. By this time, the section running from Fort Hill Square North to State Street had been substantially completed. However, the erection of steel to the north—from State Street to Commercial Street—was delayed because of complex ramp construction. The work had just started when this photograph was taken. (STL.)

LOOKING NORTH FROM NEAR STATE STREET, JANUARY 1955. In this view, steel is going up between completed sections of viaduct. Steel box girders have been placed atop concrete piers as the viaduct continues north past a blank facade at the end of Mercantile Row to the east. (STL.)

PROGRESS PHOTOGRAPH OF STEEL ROADWAY DECK FROM MILK STREET, OCTOBER 1954. Just south of this point, the Central Artery turned off Atlantic Avenue and ran farther inland through the northern section of the city's old financial district. The Grain and Wheat Exchange building, built in 1892, is on the far right. The U.S. Appraisers Stores building on Atlantic Avenue, with its crenelated roof parapet, is visible in the distance. (STL.)

THE SAME VIEW TWO MONTHS LATER. Workers lay steel reinforcing bars before pouring the concrete roadway deck. (STL.)

71

Looking North from Broad Street, July 1954. This view shows several blank facades of buildings truncated by the Central Artery demolition. In many cases, work on the Central Artery was severely slowed by the necessity of shoring up and weatherproofing these former interior walls to prevent collapse. This was a particular problem in the downtown's oldest sections between State and High Streets. (STL.)

Three Men Who Built the Central Artery. From left to right are Edgar W. Kumpel (resident engineer of the Massachusetts DPW), John B. Wilbur (head of the MIT Department of Civil Engineering and consultant to the Artery design team), and Cranston R. Rogers (chief structural engineer on the southern portion of the Artery). (Courtesy Cranston Rogers.)

Looking East over Atlantic Avenue from above the Grain and Wheat Exchange Building, Summer 1952. The point where the Central Artery swings off Atlantic Avenue farther west into downtown is clearly visible. Demolition along Atlantic Avenue has nearly been completed, with only the building at center on India Square still to be razed. Across Fort Point Channel from Rowes Wharf, the Fan Pier area is visible. Today the site of the federal courthouse, Fan Pier in this view is laced with railroad tracks and freight warehouses. Until the Central Artery was completed, shipment of goods in and out of the city was most easily accomplished by rail. Once the Artery penetrated downtown's maze of streets, however, trucks quickly became the preferred mode of shipment. (Photograph by Leslie Jones; courtesy CA/T Archives.)

LOOKING NORTH ALONG ATLANTIC AVENUE, FEBRUARY 1954. Although construction would not start until the spring, demolition of the buildings that once occupied the empty lots in front of Fort Hill Square (lower left) had been completed in 1952. This view gives some idea of the vehicular congestion that afflicted Atlantic Avenue before the Central Artery was put up. (Photograph by Leslie Jones; courtesy CA/T Archives.)

STEEL BEING ERECTED NEAR HIGH STREET, JULY 1954. The handsome brick office building in the foreground at 200 High Street still stands today. In the background, the ten-story 166 High Street office building stands at the western end of Fort Hill Square. (STL.)

AN EARLY VIEW OF THE POINT WHERE THE CENTRAL ARTERY TURNED OFF ATLANTIC AVENUE. From this point just north of Fort Hill Square, the Artery tore through the heart of the city. In the distance is the swath of destruction making its way north before turning northwest at Commercial Street in front of Mercantile Row near what is today Christopher Columbus Park. (STL.)

THE ARTERY POURS THROUGH DOWNTOWN, OCTOBER 1954. This fine view shows the state of downtown at the height of Artery construction. Vehicles, rubble, and construction materials littered large portions of the city, and construction noise echoed throughout the financial district. Note the broken and taped windows on 200 High Street on the left. (STL.)

LOOKING NORTH FROM ATLANTIC AVENUE, SEPTEMBER 1954. The raw face of 200 High Street is visible in this view, as are the old granite curbs marking where the western edge of Atlantic Avenue once was. The Custom House Tower stands a few blocks to the north. (STL.)

FOUNDATION WALL ALONG ATLANTIC AVENUE, JUNE 1955. To the right of center is the ornate Rowes Wharf building. The storefront marquees give some idea of the variety of commercial activities along this portion of the old Atlantic Avenue. The top floors of the Rowes Wharf building were used as warehouse space until it was demolished in the early 1960s. The new Rowes Wharf building, with a similar arch, was not built until 1987. (STL.)

NEW UTILITY LINES BEING LAID IN FRONT OF THE ROWES WHARF WAREHOUSE BUILDING.
Billy Vigor's Surplus, which vacated Rowes Wharf in the early 1960s upon its demolition,
reopened for business along Summer Street in Downtown Crossing before closing for good in
1998. (STL.)

LOOKING NORTH ON ATLANTIC AVENUE, SEPTEMBER 1955. On the far right, note the street
sign pointing north along Atlantic Avenue to the Mystic River Bridge; before the opening of
the Central Artery, Atlantic Avenue was the major north-south thoroughfare through the city.
The Union Freight track spur curving off to the lower right ran over the Northern Avenue
Bridge across Fort Point Channel and into the sprawling freight yards on Fan Pier. (STL.)

A WALL TO THE CITY, JULY 1955. Wooden formwork is in place before the pouring of a concrete retaining wall that will form one side of an entrance ramp. Although the ramp provided easy access to the expressway from Atlantic Avenue, it also completely cut the Rowes Wharf block off from the rest of the city. (STL.)

LOOKING EAST ACROSS THE STEEL VIADUCT AT THE ROWES WHARF BLOCK, OCTOBER 1955. Just visible above the hulking steel structure is the ornate cupola of the abandoned Boston-Revere Beach-Lynn Railroad. The railroad's northbound service had begun as a ferry ride across Boston harbor to a terminal in East Boston. When the Atlantic Avenue elevated ceased its service in 1938, the line's ridership dropped off dramatically. The line lapsed into bankruptcy and was abandoned in 1940. (STL.)

Steel Erection in October 1955, Seen from the Roof of the U.S. Appraisers Stores Building. Here, deck beams are being positioned as riveters stand by to fix them in place. Also note the grading work on the earth-filled entrance ramp in the lower right corner. (STL.)

THE STEEL EXPRESSWAY VIADUCT TURNING OFF ATLANTIC AVENUE AT HIGH STREET, NOVEMBER 1955. In this fine overview, the High Street exit ramp is already in operation for southbound traffic. In the foreground, an earth-filled ramp forms the gradual transition from elevated steel viaduct to underground roadway. (STL.)

THE VIADUCT A MONTH LATER. The steel structure is complete, and the Atlantic Avenue entrance ramp is open for northbound traffic. The High Street exit ramp on the left remained in place until the early 1990s, when it was removed to make way for International Place Phase II. Subsequently, a small addition to 200 High Street was also tacked onto the formerly blank facade of the old building. (STL.)

THE REMAINDER OF FORT HILL SQUARE, APRIL 1955. This lone streetlight once stood over a branch of High Street at Fort Hill Square's eastern edge. The buildings at the far side of the square were demolished the year after this photograph was taken to make way for a 12-story parking garage. Today this is the site of International Place Phase II, completed in 1991. (STL.)

LOOKING EAST FROM THE INTERSECTION OF OLIVER AND HIGH STREETS AT THE WESTERN EDGE OF FORT HILL SQUARE, SEPTEMBER 1955. The High Street ramp has replaced several brick office buildings and the Boston Ladder Company No. 8, which lined the northern side of Fort Hill Square. (STL.)

INDIA PLACE ROADWAY GRADING, MAY 1955. At the base of the city's majestic Grain and Wheat Exchange building, a power shovel prepares the roadway for resurfacing. This area was once the very heart of Boston's financial district. The truncated rows of brick structures along Milk and Central Streets are visible in the background. (STL.)

OLD MEETS NEW ON INDIA STREET. Looking west into downtown, this view shows the eastern end of India Street being paved with blacktop, while a section of Atlantic Avenue in the foreground still shows its original cobblestones. The street sign at left indicates an intersection with Export Street, which ceased to exist after area streets were reconfigured as part of the Central Artery construction. (STL.)

AERIAL VIEW FROM THE SOUTH OF THE BLOCK BETWEEN ATLANTIC AVENUE AND PURCHASE STREET AFTER DEMOLITION. At the top of the image, the Artery is nearly completed as far south as Fort Hill Square, now little more than a barren patch of earth in the shadow of the exit ramp. To the west of Purchase Street (center left) is the parcel soon to house the Traveler's Insurance Building, completed in 1964 and imploded in 1988. Construction halted at this point while the debate raged over which path the Artery would take farther south near Chinatown. (Courtesy CA/T Archives.)

LOOKING NORTH FROM THE ROOF OF SOUTH STATION AS THE BLOCK BETWEEN ATLANTIC AVENUE AND PURCHASE STREET COMES DOWN. The bleak landscape of cleared lots is a stark contrast to the downtown skyline, which had not changed significantly since 1930, when the United Shoe Machinery Building (upper left) was completed. The covered corner of the Wentworth Building (lower left, facing Dewey Square) had been the center of activity for the throngs of newsboys and "play takers" who frequented the square by day. (Photograph by Leslie Jones; courtesy Boston Public Library, Prints Department.)

Looking South with Dewey Square in the Distance, Spring 1956. This remarkable view shows the massive scale of demolition that preceded the construction of the Central Artery tunnel. As dictated by the 1948 Highway Master Plan, the Central Artery absorbed the

blocks between Atlantic Avenue (left) and Purchase Street. On the right is the city's first office skyscraper, the United Shoe Machinery Building, completed in 1929. To the right of center is the cleared lot that would become the Traveler's Insurance Building. (Courtesy William Litant.)

LOOKING SOUTH FROM OLIVER STREET TOWARD DEWEY SQUARE, APRIL 1956. Demolition of buildings to the north of Dewey Square in the path of the tunnel has been completed, and excavation is just beginning in the vicinity of Congress Street. The eight-story Brown Building at the far side of Dewey Square is prominent. (STL.)

LOOKING NORTH FROM DEWEY SQUARE, APRIL 1956. The block between Atlantic Avenue and Purchase Street has been replaced by a muddy ditch nearly 200 feet wide. (STL.)

LOOKING NORTH FROM CONGRESS STREET WITH ROWES WHARF IN THE BACKGROUND, MAY 1956. In this view, work is progressing on the expressway's transition ramp. Workers are placing waterproofing material atop a layer of drainage bricks in the shadow of the old Boston Post building on Purchase Street. (STL.)

STEEL SHEET PILES BEING DRIVEN JUST SOUTH OF CONGRESS STREET, JUNE 1956. These piles were necessary to prevent the walls of the tunnel trench from collapsing or neighboring buildings from subsiding. These buildings along Atlantic Avenue were cleared in 1971 as part of a plan by the Boston Redevelopment Authority to renew the area around South Station—a plan that initially included demolition of the station building. (STL.)

THE TUNNEL'S TRANSITION RAMPS, JUNE 1956. Here, the ramps have been formed and poured, and the tunnel face has reached Congress Street. Several of the buildings on the right still stand today, wedged between skyscrapers. (STL.)

LOOKING SOUTH TOWARD SUMMER STREET FROM CONGRESS STREET, JUNE 1956. DPW Commissioner John Volpe (later governor) directed the Central Artery tunnel west of most of the city's leather district, the area in the center of this image. However, the eight-story Brown Building, built in 1900 at the corner of Summer Street and Atlantic Avenue, fell victim to the tunnel's trench. (STL.)

DEWEY SQUARE FOUR MONTHS LATER. In this view looking northwest up Federal Street, the nearly demolished Brown Building is on the left. An entrance to the MTA station underneath Dewey Square is visible at right in front of the Cafeteria Albiani. (Photograph by Leslie Jones; courtesy Boston Public Library, Prints Department.)

WORKERS PREPARING FORMWORK BEFORE PLACING CONCRETE, OCTOBER 1956. The Brown Building has been completely razed. The Massachusetts Envelope Company building is now the site of One Financial Center, and the old Hotel Essex is just visible on Atlantic Avenue, which curves to the left. (STL.)

LOOKING NORTH FROM DEWEY SQUARE, JULY 1956. The steel framework of the tunnel takes shape as the expressway tunnel cuts a swath between Atlantic Avenue and Purchase Street. In the distance, an MTA bus runs north along Congress Street toward downtown. (STL.)

THE TUNNEL'S STEEL FRAMEWORK JUST NORTH OF DEWEY SQUARE, JULY 1956. At the time of its construction, the tunnel was the widest traffic tunnel anywhere in the world. Its cost was $15 million. (STL.)

LOOKING ACROSS DEWEY SQUARE FROM THE TOP OF THE HOTEL ESSEX, JULY 1956. The tunnel's steel frame now occupies the 200-foot-wide trench that replaced the block between Atlantic Avenue and Purchase Street. Congress Street is to the right of center, at the northern end of the tunnel, and the Rowes Wharf building is just visible in the upper right corner. (Photograph by Leslie Jones; courtesy CA/T Archives.)

LOOKING NORTH FROM DEWEY SQUARE, OCTOBER 1956. With the tunnel framework complete, a concrete topping slab is poured atop the roof beams. A 1953 engineering report advocated creating a new surface road atop the depressed expressway, suggesting that the new boulevard would "probably become the finest street in Downtown Boston." (STL.)

THE BLANK FACADE OF THE HECHT BUILDING, OCTOBER 1956. The Hecht Building was home to the Massachusetts Envelope Company. It is shown after the demolition of abutting buildings and the Brown Building. South Station is on the left. (STL.)

EXCAVATION WORK PROCEEDING IN FRONT OF SOUTH STATION, DECEMBER 1956. This area had been the edge of Boston Harbor until the mid 19th century, and the shallow water table made excavation a muddy endeavor. The entire block of buildings opposite South Station in this view was demolished in 1971 to make way for the Federal Reserve Tower. (Courtesy Peter Vanderwarker and CA/T Archives.)

LOOKING EAST ACROSS DEWEY SQUARE TOWARD SOUTH STATION. The Central Artery tunnel was cut about 100 yards in front of South Station between Atlantic Avenue and Purchase Street. In this view, a trench for Boston Edison lines has been formed below the grade of the roadway to accommodate relocated utilities. (STL.)

DEMOLITION OF THE OLD DEWEY SQUARE MTA CAMBRIDGE-DORCHESTER RAPID TRANSIT STATION LOBBY, FEBRUARY 1957. Built between 1912 and 1917, the line (now the MBTA Red Line) ran underground from Harvard Station south to Ashmont Station. The Dewey Square station was relocated closer to South Station. (Courtesy Peter Vanderwarker and CA/T Archives.)

UNDER DEWEY SQUARE, APRIL 1957. This fascinating image gives some idea of the extent of subterranean complexities facing Central Artery tunnel contractors around Dewey Square. To the left of center is the top of the MTA tunnel with its new flat roof. Just above that, a 4-foot diameter brick sewer line has been cut, and various other utility lines stud the excavation face at various points. (STL.)

DEMOLITION OF THE MTA
TUNNEL ROOF, MARCH 1957.
Visible in the background is
Summer Street, extending north
into downtown. This section of
the MTA tunnel's roof arch had
to be demolished and made flush
with the bottom of the excavation
trench to allow room for the
Central Artery tunnel to pass over
it. (Courtesy Peter Vanderwarker
and CA/T Archives.)

LOOKING DOWN THE MTA SUBWAY TUNNEL AT DEWEY SQUARE. This image shows the
reconstructed roof where the Central Artery tunnel passed overhead. The new steel-framed
roof was constructed before demolition began on the old arched roof to avoid disruption of
service. (Courtesy the Barletta Company.)

SUMMER STREET, JUNE 1957. Note the severed brick sewer line in the center. It is flanked by a temporary wood-encased bypass pipe, which maintained service during the construction. Steel columns forming one wall of the tunnel stand in the foreground. (STL.)

GRADING THE DEWEY SQUARE NORTHBOUND ON RAMP, JULY 1958. Clearly visible in this view is the depth of fill that covered this part of Boston. On the right, a layer of hard clay (underwater at high tide until the mid-1800s) lies about 10 feet below the filled surface of Dewey Square at this point. (STL.)

THE COMPLETED TUNNEL BOX WITH RAMPS ON EITHER SIDE AT ESSEX STREET, DECEMBER 1957. The Surface Artery would soon run atop the tunnel's roof. In addition to being the widest vehicular tunnel in the world at the time, the Central Artery tunnel was the only such tunnel to include entrance and exit ramps along its length. (STL.)

LOOKING SOUTH INTO THE NEARLY COMPLETED ARTERY TUNNEL FROM PURCHASE STREET. Rather than indicating the destination of the tunnel, "Bethlehem" refers to the steel fabrication company that furnished the steel for the job. (STL.)

THE ESSEX STREET VENT BUILDING UNDER CONSTRUCTION BEHIND THE HOTEL ESSEX, JANUARY 1958. Ventilation of the Central Artery tunnel was to be achieved by huge fan enclosures placed alongside the tunnel route. Future Massachusetts Secretary of Transportation Frederick Salvucci, an instrumental figure in planning and implementing the depression of the elevated expressway, worked as a laborer on a similar vent building in high school. (STL.)

THE SUMMER STREET VENT BUILDING UNDER CONSTRUCTION, FEBRUARY 1958. Ventilation fans exhausted stale air from the tunnel through these stacks, while fresh air was drawn in through the tunnel's end portals and ramp openings. (STL.)

CLEARING RUBBLE IN THE VICINITY OF BEACH STREET, JULY 1956. As the area north of Dewey Square was razed in the summer and fall of 1956, demolition was also proceeding to the south. In this view, the handsome stone and brick building on Essex Street is next in line. On the left, exposed facades of lofts on Kingston and Edinboro Streets are prominent. (STL.)

DEMOLITION IN THE VICINITY OF LINCOLN STREET IN THE CITY'S LEATHER DISTRICT, SEPTEMBER 1956. Although this area was spared from the blight of the elevated expressway, Artery tunnel construction necessitated the demolition of everything in its path. The ornate Lincoln Building, erected in 1895 and still standing today, is visible on the right. (STL.)

WORKERS DEMOLISHING A PIECE OF THE CITY PARKING GARAGE ON ESSEX STREET IN THE LEATHER DISTRICT. Great care was taken to demolish only a small fraction of the garage structure, unlike most other buildings that stood only partially in the path of the Artery tunnel. Planners recognized that the new highway would place enormous demands on the city's parking facilities, and the garage was one of the few parking structures in the city. By 1960, several additional parking garages had been built nearby to meet the increased demand. (Photograph by Leslie Jones; courtesy Boston Public Library, Prints Department.)

A Demolition Worker Standing amid the Rubble of the City Garage. The majority of the demolition work in the southern portion of the project was performed by the J.J. Duane Company, the area's largest demolition contractor at the time. The period between 1950 and 1970 was an excellent time to be in the demolition business in Boston—during those years, almost one-quarter of the city's downtown area was cleared for highway or urban renewal projects. (Photograph by Leslie Jones; courtesy Boston Public Library, Prints Department.)

LOOKING NORTH FROM BEACH STREET, OCTOBER 1956. What once was a block of brick warehouse buildings along Kingston Street is now a gaping trench nearly 150 feet wide. The Central Artery tunnel, the widest in the world at the time, was also the most destructive. (STL.)

ANOTHER VIEW ALMOST A MONTH LATER. In this photograph, steel columns have been erected to form the tunnel's walls. The truncation of the two-story city parking garage (top center) has nearly been completed. (STL.)

SNOW COVERING THE TUNNEL TRENCH, JANUARY 1957. The tunnel is approaching its narrowest point along Albany Street in Chinatown. The three-story Chinese Merchants Association Building (with the pagoda-style cupola) is being reframed as steelwork proceeds behind it. (STL.)

TUNNEL CONSTRUCTION BETWEEN ESSEX AND BEACH STREETS AT THE EASTERN EDGE OF CHINATOWN, APRIL 1957. This image shows several phases of the "cut and cover" method of tunneling. Once demolition of all surface structures had been completed, a huge trench was dug and shored. A steel and concrete roof covering the tunnel was then constructed, filled over, and paved to form a surface street. (STL.)

POURING THE ROAD DECK INSIDE THE ARTERY TUNNEL NEAR BEACH STREET, APRIL 1958. The floor of the Central Artery tunnel consisted of a 3-foot-thick concrete slab poured between steel beams, which gave the tunnel box rigidity. This mass of concrete counteracted the tendency for the tunnel box to become buoyant atop the shallow water table. (STL.)

GRADING AND EXCAVATION WORK ON ALBANY STREET, MARCH 1957. The tunnel excavation required demolishing half of the Albany Street–Hudson Street block, exposing the shantied rear lots of the buildings that fronted on Hudson Street (right). Scaffolding cloaks the Chinese Merchants Association Building (top right), where a new stone exterior is being installed after half of the building was cut off. (STL.)

Looking South along Albany Street at the Artery Tunnel's Narrowest Point, June 1957. DPW Commissioner John Volpe had promised to minimize the tunnel's impact in the Chinatown neighborhood. He left his successor, Anthony DiNatale, a tight squeeze at Albany and Kneeland Streets between the Chinese Merchants Association Building and the Albany Building, which occupied the entire block on the opposite side of the street. (STL.)

Excavation Work along Albany Street, May 1958. In a view looking over the tunnel's roof beams, the cupola of the Chinese Merchants Association Building is visible in the upper right corner. The building has a new stone exterior, erasing any outward scars left by Artery construction. These buildings remain today, without the tin shacks. (STL.)

EXCAVATING BY HAND AT THE BASE OF THE CHINESE MERCHANTS ASSOCIATION BUILDING ON ALBANY STREET, JUNE 1958. The wooden support bracing held the Chinese Merchants Association Building up while permanent foundations were under construction. (STL.)

BRACING AT THE ALBANY BUILDING, JULY 1958. These workers are placing waterproofing sheets along the outer edge of the tunnel wall. The sign on the Albany Building at upper right reads, "Pardon our appearance during excavation," and directs customers to a door that hangs precariously out over the massive tunnel trench. (STL.)

AN OPERATOR WITH HIS CRANE IN FRONT OF THE CHINESE MERCHANTS ASSOCIATION BUILDING, SUMMER 1958. The general contractor for the entire downtown portion of the Central Artery was the Barletta Company, based in Roslindale. Founded in 1913 by Italian immigrant Vincenzo Barletta, the Barletta Company had undertaken several earlier highway projects around the city, including the East Boston Expressway in 1952. Today the company is run by Vincenzo's three great-grandsons—Christopher Barletta, Timothy Barletta, and Vincent Barletta Jr. (STL.)

EXCAVATION WORK ON KNEELAND STREET, OCTOBER 1958. The relocation of utilities around the Central Artery tunnel required extensive excavation work on surrounding streets during the nearly three years of construction. The pipe at the center of the image is being temporarily supported by a cable as excavation proceeds beneath it. (STL.)

LOOKING NORTH TOWARD CHINATOWN AND THE LEATHER DISTRICT. Shown here is the southern approach to the unexcavated tunnel section under Kneeland Street. In the background are the Chinese Merchants Association Building and the Albany Building. (STL.)

INSIDE THE COMPLETED EXPRESSWAY TUNNEL UNDER CONGRESS STREET, NOVEMBER 1958.
The walls of the tunnel were tiled in pale yellow, and continuous rows of fluorescent lighting were designed to minimize the eyestrain associated with passing from daylight to tunnel light while driving. (STL.)

ANOTHER VIEW INSIDE THE COMPLETED EXPRESSWAY TUNNEL. This photograph shows a bank of ventilation fans beside the roadway. These fans pull stale air out of the tunnel and exhaust it from two vent buildings, shown on page 100. (STL.)

INSIDE THE TUNNEL CONTROL ROOM, COMPLETED IN THE SUMMER OF 1959. From this room, a single operator could monitor traffic conditions inside the tunnel and dispatch help in the event of an accident or stranded motorist. Unfortunately, the primitive electronics produced a tremendous amount of heat, and the control room was furnished with neither windows nor an air-conditioning system. Conditions proved intolerable to DPW operators, and without funds to install air conditioning, the system fell into disuse. (STL.)

LOOKING NORTH FROM THE BOSTON AND ALBANY RAILROAD'S SOUTHERN FREIGHT YARD TOWARD KNEELAND STREET, MARCH 1957. Two freight houses and four tracks were demolished to make way for the Central Artery. The 14-story Hudson Building in Chinatown is visible on the left. (STL.)

ROUGH GRADING IN THE SOUTH BAY FREIGHT YARDS, JULY 1957. The massive Boston and Albany Freight House No. 1 survived another seven years before being demolished to make way for Massachusetts Turnpike Extension ramps. The twin smokestacks of the Boston Edison Illuminating Company's plant, built in 1931, dominate the background. (STL.)

LOOKING NORTH FROM OAK STREET ALONG ALBANY STREET, SPRING 1957. The back windows of these apartment buildings fronting on Hudson Street once faced a narrow lightwell between a similar set of apartment buildings along Albany Street. Within a few years, residents of these apartments would be afforded front row views of one of the busiest expressways in the northeastern United States. (STL.)

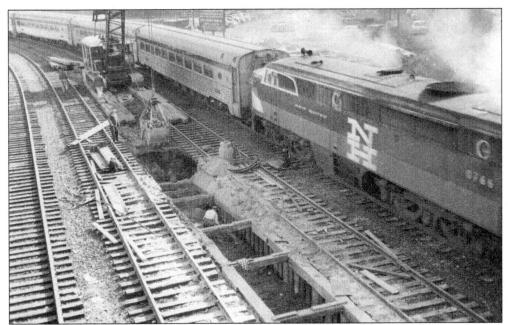

EXCAVATING THE SOUTHERN VIADUCT'S FOUNDATION AMID TRACKS OF THE NEW YORK, NEW HAVEN AND HARTFORD RAILROAD, NOVEMBER 1957. This scene illustrates a pattern repeated nationwide in the late 1950s—express highways replacing railways as the favored means of intercity passenger travel. (STL.)

A REMINDER OF BOSTON'S PAST, OCTOBER 1957. Shown near the intersection of Albany and Berkeley Streets at the southern end of Fort Point Channel, these wooden pilings were once part of an ocean pier. They were filled over as the city's South Bay region shrank in the first quarter of the 20th century. The pilings made excavation particularly complex, as they proved extremely difficult to extract. (STL.)

LOOKING EAST ACROSS THE NEW HAVEN RAIL YARDS TOWARD THE DOMINO SUGAR REFINERY, SEPTEMBER 1957. Piles are being driven as part of the southern viaduct's foundation. The Domino plant was built during World War I and ceased operations shortly before this photograph was taken. The plant was demolished in late 1957, and the land was sold to the Gillette Company, which subsequently built its current manufacturing plant on the site. (STL.)

TESTING A PILE COLUMN, NOVEMBER 1957. Boston's unpredictable soil conditions—especially in filled areas south of Summer Street—made it necessary to test each load-bearing column with a device such as this one to ensure structural soundness. The workman is hand-pumping a hydraulic jack and will record movement of the pile. (STL.)

LOOKING NORTH OVER THE REBUILT BROADWAY BRIDGE, JUNE 1957. The Boston and Albany Railroad tracks swing to the north in the distance, and the Dorchester Avenue Bridge is to the right. At the upper left is the massive U.S. Postal Annex at South Station. (STL.)

LOOKING WEST UP DOVER (NOW EAST BERKELEY) STREET, SUMMER 1958. The area north of Dover Street had just fallen victim to the Boston Redevelopment Authority's urban renewal plans. Dubbed the "New York Streets" neighborhood (its streets bore the names of New York State's Native American tribes), it was home to a diverse mix of working-class families before being razed to make way for industrial uses. (STL.)

116

HOISTING STEEL GIRDERS INTO PLACE OVER THE BOSTON AND ALBANY RAILROAD TRACKS, AUGUST 1958. In the background is the Albany Street Bridge. On the right, another girder waits its turn. (STL.)

THE DOVER STREET BRIDGE FARTHER SOUTH, LOOKING EAST TOWARD SOUTH BOSTON OVER FORT POINT CHANNEL. The massive Gillette plant on the left, built in 1923, still stands today next to a more modern facility. The large industrial building just south of the Gillette facility is the Court Square Press. (STL.)

117

THE SOUTHERN VIADUCT TAKING SHAPE OVER THE BOSTON AND ALBANY RAILROAD TRACKS, SUMMER 1958. This area, near the intersection of Broadway and Albany Street, would undergo a major transformation when William Callahan, a former DPW chairman, brought the Massachusetts Turnpike into downtown in 1964, eradicating the old residential neighborhood in the upper left corner. (STL.)

THE NEARLY COMPLETED VIADUCT ALMOST A YEAR LATER. In the distance is the completed Dewey Square tunnel's southern portal as well as the truncated Chinese Merchants Association Building and Albany Building. (STL.)

FILLING IN PART OF THE SOUTH BAY MUD FLATS, NOVEMBER 1957. To minimize property damage, DPW planners routed the expressway along the banks of the city's South Bay—a muddy backwater at the southern extremity of Fort Point Channel. In an era before federally mandated environmental impact reviews, such areas could be filled at the discretion of the DPW. (STL.)

LOOKING SOUTH TOWARD DORCHESTER, JULY 1958. This image shows the extent of new filling at the southern end of Fort Point Channel with Albany Street on the right. In the distance is the massive gasoline storage tank of the Boston Consolidated Gas Company at the southern end of Massachusetts Avenue. (STL.)

ENGINEERS FROM THE DEMATTEO CONSTRUCTION COMPANY ATOP THE COLUMBIA ROAD OVERPASS, DECEMBER 1958. A section of roadway can be seen in the distance. The link to the Southeast Expressway was fully completed on June 25, 1959, marking the end of the Central Artery project. The DPW paid DeMatteo an extra $1 million to accelerate work on the southern section of roadway in order to finish by June 30—the date set by the New York, New Haven and Hartford Railroad to abandon their commuter passenger service to the southern suburbs. With the Central Artery's completion imminent, the state legislature cut off its subsidy to the railroad in 1958, dooming its passenger service. (STL.)

Three

BOSTON AFTER THE ARTERY

LOOKING SOUTH TOWARD CAUSEWAY STREET ALONG A NEWLY REPAVED BEVERLY STREET, OCTOBER 1955. This type of dismal streetscape became all too familiar to Bostonians over the next several decades. (STL.)

BOSTON AFTER THE ARTERY, FROM HIGH ABOVE SOUTH STATION, 1960. This view shows the tremendous swath cut through the city by the elevated roadway, with North Station at the upper left and Dewey Square at the lower left. The amputation of the North End from the rest of the city is all too evident, and the waterfront is neatly cut off from the downtown area. This image captures the city on the brink of massive demolition at the hands of the Boston Redevelopment Authority's urban renewal program. Already a small piece of the old Scollay Square has been razed on the left. This photograph was taken as part of a waterfront redevelopment proposal and identifies each of the city's major wharves. (Courtesy BRA Archives/Peter Vanderwarker.)

BOSTON IN THE MID-1960S. This photograph shows the effects of urban renewal as well as the tremendous swath cut through the city by the Artery. On the right, the West End and Scollay Square have been razed, and construction is proceeding on a number of office buildings and residential towers in their place. The view also vividly illustrates the Artery's effect on Chinatown and the leather district, visible on the left near South Station. (Courtesy CA/T Archives.)

ONE ELEVATED STRUCTURE MEETING ANOTHER OVER CAUSEWAY STREET, OCTOBER 1955. The elevated railway viaduct, built in 1901, is dwarfed by the new expressway. The lone woman gives scale to the structures. (STL.)

124

HAYMARKET SQUARE AFTER THE ARTERY, NOVEMBER 1955. This view shows what remained of Haymarket Square after its northern half was sacrificed for the Central Artery. Of particular note are the old streetcar tracks still set in Washington Street (lower right), superseded in 1901 by the construction of the Tremont Street Subway extension, which emerged from its tunnel just north of the square. (Courtesy William Litant.)

HAYMARKET SQUARE, DECEMBER 1954. This bleak urban landscape was what remained of the North End's primary commercial district. Of particular interest is the sign on the extreme left urging local residents to vote republican. Considering that the Central Artery program was jump-started in 1948 by Republican Governor Bradford, its appeal seems doubtful. (STL.)

LOOKING NORTH UP BLACKSTONE STREET FROM NORTH STREET, NOVEMBER 1955. The market stalls on the left are all that remain of the old open-air market area. The appeal of the open-air market seems dubious considering the proximity of the expressway. A period newspaper called this the city's "rejuvenated market area." (STL.)

CROSS STREET, LOOKING NORTH FROM HANOVER STREET. This image, with the new Central Artery on the left, also shows the results of a prior path of demolition through the North End. The one-story shops along the north side of Cross Street sprang up after the 1933 widening of the street left pieces of cleared lots on the north side of the street. Eventually, shop owners reclaimed the unused parcels and erected small commercial spaces. (STL.)

THE COMPLETED ATLANTIC AVENUE ENTRY RAMP. This ramp passes directly in front of what was at the time one of Boston's most architecturally diverse and notable blocks, stretching along Atlantic Avenue from Northern Avenue to India Wharf. The ramp was removed as part of the current Central Artery/Tunnel project, slated for completion in 2004. (STL.)

LOOKING SOUTH FROM SOUTH STREET ALONG THE NEWLY PAVED SURFACE ROAD SITTING ATOP THE ARTERY TUNNEL. Hardly becoming the "finest street in downtown Boston" as once predicted, the surface road today is one of the city's greatest pedestrian hazards. The old adage that Dewey Square got its name from a weary pedestrian asking "Do we or don't we dare cross?" still rings true. (STL.)

THE SOUTHERN PORTAL OF THE ARTERY TUNNEL, JULY 1959. The Chinese Merchants Association Building and Albany Building still stand today. The freight truck on the left is evidence of one of the Central Artery's effects on the city of Boston—downtown wholesalers and manufacturers favoring truck service over the railroad for delivery of goods and raw materials. (STL.)

LOOKING NORTH OVER THE COMPLETED SOUTHERN VIADUCT AT THE INTERSECTION OF ALBANY STREET AND BROADWAY, JULY 1959. Traffic on the Central Artery looks light five days after it was opened for traffic. Only three months later, a "temporary bottleneck" caused a massive traffic jam that tied up the northbound Artery during the evening commute. It was an omen of things to come. (STL.)

CPSIA information can be obtained
at www.ICGtesting.com
Printed in the USA
BVOW07*1633050318
509717BV00013B/1102/P